cloverleaf books™

Money Basics

Lily Learns about Wants and Needs

Lisa Bullard

illustrated by **Christine M. Schneider**

M MILLBROOK PRESS • MINNEAPOLIS

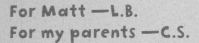

For Matt —L.B.
For my parents —C.S.

Millbrook Press
A division of Lerner Publishing Group, Inc.
241 First Avenue North
Minneapolis, MN 55401 U.S.A.

Website address: www.lernerbooks.com

Main body text set in Slappy Inline 18/28.
Typeface provided by T26.

Library of Congress Cataloging-in-Publication Data

Bullard, Lisa.
    Lily learns about wants and needs / Lisa Bullard ; illustrated by Christine Schneider.
        p.   cm. — (Cloverleaf books™ — money basics)
    Includes index.
    ISBN 978–1–4677–0764–0 (lib. bdg. : alk. paper)
    ISBN 978–1–4677–1698–7 (eBook)
    1. Budgets, Personal—Juvenile literature. 2. Consumption (Economics)—Juvenile literature. I. Schneider, Christine, 1971– illustrator. II. Schneider, Christine, illustrator. III. Title.
HG179.B8193 2014
332.024—dc23   2012045896

Manufactured in the United States of America
1 – BP – 7/15/13

TABLE OF CONTENTS

Chapter One

Want or Need?

"Hey, Dad! You want me to watch less **TV** and play outside more. So I really **need** this new bike," I said.

"You might **want** a new bike, Lily," Dad said. "But that's not the same as needing one. A 'need' is something we have to have."

Dad thought a moment. "We all **need** to exercise. But you can ride your old bike. Or do other active things."

"So can I buy a skateboard? Or roller skates?" I asked.

Dad smiled. "Good try! But today, let's only spend money on things we **need**."

What is something you want but don't need?

Chapter Two

Buying Only What We Need

"**I need** a new raincoat," I said. "My old one is too small. I like that one."

"Rainy season is coming soon," Dad said. "Let's check it out."

Dad looked at the coat and the price tag. "This won't keep you very dry. And it costs too much. We'll keep looking."

I found another raincoat on sale. Dad let me buy that one.

Are the things that cost the most always the best choices?

"Time for your visit to the dentist," said Dad. "We're only spending money on things we **need**," I said. "So we don't have to go. My teeth have already fallen out!"

Dad laughed. "Sorry, Lily. You **need** to see the dentist anyway."

"I was good at the dentist," I said. "Can we go bowling? Or play mini golf?"

Dad shook his head. "We have to pay for those. But the park is free."

I swung high on the swings. Then I saw the ice cream truck. "Dad, I'm hungry. I really **need** some ice cream!"

Dad said, "Special treats are okay sometimes. **But a treat is a want, not a need.** Let's find a healthy snack at the grocery store on our way home."

What is your favorite healthy snack?

Chapter Three
Everyone Has to Make Choices

At the store, Dad took out a shopping list. "Deciding about **wants** and **needs** isn't just for kids. Our whole family has to do it. Want to help?"

I looked at the list. "Mom always says **I need** to drink my milk. And eat my vegetables. So I guess we have to get them. And we **need** toilet paper!" I took another look. "Dad, you wrote *root beer* in big red letters. Does that mean we need it?"

Dad looked sad. "I love root beer," he said. **"But it's a 'want,' not a 'need.'** We'll skip it today."

GROCERIES
toilet paper
milk
apples
peas
soup
green beans
carrots
cereal
soup
ROOT BEER
rice
crackers

What does your family need besides healthful food and water?

15

Mom works at the hospital. We stopped to pick her up.

"What are the things that people in the hospital **need?**" Dad asked me.

"Help from doctors," I said. "And medicine."
Dad said, "Right."

"Think hard," Dad said. "What does the hospital have that people don't really need but might **want?**"
I couldn't come up with anything.

"I know," said Mom. "The rooms all have TVs. People like to watch them. But people don't need TV to get better."

"TV makes me feel better!" I said. "But Dad wants me to ride my old bike instead."

What do you need when you feel sick?

When "Wants" Are Okay

Dad had an idea as we drove home. "Sometimes after people buy all they **need**, they have money left over. Then they can buy something they **want**. How about tomorrow we ride our bikes back to the park? We'll buy ice cream!"

"Good idea, Dad," I said. "Because I know you think ice cream is a 'want.' But my stomach sure thinks it's a 'need!'"

Make a Needs and Wants Poster

Are you still trying to tell needs apart from wants? Making this poster might help you decide which is which.

What you need:

Large sheet of paper   Old magazines, catalogs,   Scissors
Color crayons   or newspapers   Glue or tape

What you do:

1) Draw a line from left to right across the middle of your sheet of paper. Draw another line from top to bottom across the middle of the paper. When you are finished, your paper will be divided into four squares.

2) Write NEEDS in three of the squares. Write WANTS in the last square.

3) Look through your magazines and catalogs. Cut out pictures of things that are needs. This might include:
   - healthful food
   - soap
   - toothpaste
   - sunscreen
   - a house or an apartment
   - a winter jacket
   - medicine

   As you cut out the needs, glue or tape the pictures onto the NEEDS sections of your poster.

4) Go back through the magazines and catalogs. This time, choose some items that are wants. Remember, the WANTS section of your paper is much smaller. Most people cannot have everything they want! You might have to make hard choices. Glue or tape your choices onto the WANTS section of your poster.

GLOSSARY

choices: different things that you can pick from

medicine: something used to cure illness or make sick people feel better

need: when you must have something to be safe or healthy; or the thing that you must have

want: when you wish or would like to have something; or the thing that you wish for

ANSWER KEY

page 9: No

page 15: Families also need things such as a place to live, clothes to wear, and a way to get from one place to another.

BOOKS

Larson, Jennifer S. *Do I Need It? Or Do I Want It?: Making Budget Choices.*
Minneapolis: Lerner Publications, 2010.
Pick up this book to learn more about wants, needs, and spending money.

Salzmann, Mary Elizabeth. *Money for Food.* Edina, MN: Magic Wagon, 2011.
Follow along in this colorful picture book as Adam makes choices about spending money
for food.

WEBSITES

It's My Life: Money
http://pbskids.org/itsmylife/money/index.html
Check out the Money section of this fun site from PBS. You'll
find information on wants and needs, along with tips on how
to earn money or manage what you have.

Planet Orange
http://www.orangekids.com
This website from ING Direct lets you blast off to play games
and learn more about making money choices.

LERNER ℮ SOURCE™
Expand learning beyond the printed book. Download free, complementary educational resources for this book from our website, www.lernersource.com.